POLAR ANIMALS

SNOWY OWLS

ARE AWESOME

by Jaclyn Jaycox

Consultant: Greg Breed
Associate Professor of Ecology
Institute of Arctic Biology
University of Alaska, Fairbanks

PEBBLE
a capstone imprint

A+ Books are published by Pebble,
1710 Roe Crest Drive, North Mankato, Minnesota 56003
www.mycapstone.com

Library of Congress Cataloging-in-Publication Data
Names: Jaycox, Jaclyn, 1983–author.
Title: Snowy Owls Are Awesome / by Jaclyn Jaycox.
Description: North Mankato, Minnesota: an imprint of Pebble, [2020] |
    Series: A+. Polar Animals | Audience: Age 4–8. | Audience: K to Grade 3. |
    Includes bibliographical references and index.
Identifiers: LCCN 2018056758 | ISBN 9781977108210 (hardcover) | ISBN
    9781977110015 (paperback) | ISBN 9781977108302 (ebook pdf)
Subjects: LCSH: Snowy owl—Juvenile literature. | Animals—Polar
    regions—Juvenile literature.
Classification: LCC QL696.S83 J39 2020 | DDC 598.9/7—dc23
LC record available at https://lccn.loc.gov/2018056758

Editorial Credits
Nikki Potts, editor; Kayla Rossow, designer; Morgan Walters, media researcher;
Laura Manthe, production specialist

Photo Credits
Newscom: Michael Dietrich imageBROKER, 22, Michio Hoshino/ Minden Pictures, 20, 23, Peltomaeki/picture alliance /blickwinkel/J, 21, Shirley Hawkes/NHPA/Photoshot, 19, Winfried Wisniewski/ Minden Pictures, 18, Wisniewski, W./picture alliance / Arco Images G, 15; Shutterstock: critterbiz, 13, David Osborn, 25, FotoRequest, Cover, 10, Frank Fichtmueller, 27, Guoqiang Xue, 12, Jim Cumming, 6, 28, Mara008, design element (blue), Milan Zygmunt, 9, MZPHOTO.CZ, 17, Oliay, design element (ice window), Paul J Hartley, 24, Paul Tessier, 8, photosoft, design element (ice), Pictureguy, 29, Stanislav Duben, 5, Stephen Lavery, 11, Todd Maertz, 7, Troutnut, 26, Wang LiQiang, 4, 14

All internet sites appearing in back matter were available and accurate when this book was sent to press.

Note to Parents, Teachers, and Librarians

This Polar Animals book uses full-color photographs and a nonfiction format to introduce the concept of snowy owls. *Snowy Owls Are Awesome* is designed to be read aloud to a pre-reader or to be read independently by an early reader. Photographs help listeners and early readers understand the text and concepts discussed. The book encourages further learning by including the following sections: Table of Contents, Glossary, Read More, Internet Sites, Critical Thinking Questions, and Index. Early readers may need assistance using these features.

TABLE OF CONTENTS

Snow White

Where does a snowy owl get its name? From its white feathers, of course! These beautiful polar birds look different from other owls. Snowy owls are the only owl with almost all white coloring.

Magnificent Owls

There are about 30,000 snowy owls in the world. They are mainly found in the Arctic. Snowy owls like treeless, wide-open areas.

Snowy owls usually stay near the ground, standing on rocks or snow. Some snowy owls stay in the Arctic all year. Others fly south for the winter.

Snowy owls are one of the largest owls. They weigh about 4 pounds (1.8 kilograms). Snowy owls have white feathers covering their bodies. Even their feet have feathers!

Females have some
brown feathers mixed in.
Feathers keep them warm.
White feathers also help
owls blend in with the snow.

Snowy owls have long wings. Their wingspan is about 5 feet (1.5 meters).

Snowy owls have black beaks and feet. Their eyes are bright yellow. Snowy owls can't move their eyes. They move their heads to look around.

On the Hunt

Snowy owls sit still for long periods of time—sometimes for hours!

Snowy owls have excellent hearing and eyesight. They can hear prey moving under the snow. When prey gets close, they dive into the snow.

Snowy owls have soft feathers. The feathers help owls fly quietly. Owls can easily sneak up on their prey. They eat lemmings. Owls also eat mice and other rodents. A snowy owl can eat up to 1,600 rodents a year!

Snowy owls hunt at night and during the day. They swallow their food whole. Then they spit up the bones and fur. Scientists study the bones and fur to learn about the owls. Snowy owls also need water. They get water from the food they eat.

Family Life

Snowy owls live alone, except during mating season. Females build nests on the ground or on rocks. They lay between three and 11 eggs.

In years when the owls
have more food to eat, they
lay more eggs. If food is
scarce, they lay fewer eggs.

Female snowy owls keep the eggs safe and warm. Baby owls hatch from the eggs after about one month.

Baby owls are called
owlets. Owlets are white
and fuzzy when they hatch.

The male owl brings food to the owlets. It also protects the nest. Owls will attack any predator that comes near. The female owl feeds the food to the owlets.

After about a month, the owlets leave the nest. They learn to fly and hunt.

Staying Safe

Snowy owls can live up to 10 years. They have few predators.

Arctic foxes and wolves
may attack owls during
nesting season. Humans
also hunt owls for sport
or for their feathers.

Earth's changing climate is harmful to an owl's prey. Lemmings need a cold climate and lots of snow to have young. Warmer weather means fewer lemmings are born. Snowy owls may have less to eat.

lemming

Snowy owls are one of
the few animals that can
live in the snowy Arctic.

They are known for their wintry-white feathers. But they are also great hunters. Not only are snowy owls beautiful, they are fierce polar animals.

GLOSSARY

Arctic (ARK-tik)—the area near the North Pole; the Arctic is cold and covered with ice

climate (KLY-muht)—the average weather of a place throughout the year

female (FEE-male)—an animal that can give birth to young animals or lay eggs

lemming (LEM-ming)—a small mammal with furry feet and a short tail

male (MALE)—an animal that can father young

mate (MATE)—to join together to produce young

polar (POH-lur)—having to do with the icy regions around the North or South Pole

predator (PRED-uh-tur)—an animal that hunts other animals for food

prey (PRAY)—an animal hunted by another animal for food

rodent (ROHD-uhnt)—a type of small mammal with long front teeth used for gnawing; rats, mice, and squirrels are rodents

scarce (SKARCE)—hard to find

wingspan (WING-span)—the distance between the tips of a pair of wings when fully open

READ MORE

Hill, Melissa. *Snowy Owls*. Owls. North Mankato, MN: Capstone Press, 2016.

Hirsch, Rebecca E. *Snowy Owls: Stealthy Hunting Birds*. Comparing Animal Traits. Minneapolis: Lerner Publications, 2016.

Lawrence, Riley. *Snowy Owls of the Tundra*. Animals of the Tundra. New York: KidHaven Publishing, 2017.

INTERNET SITES

Canadian Geographic, Animal Facts: Snowy Owls
https://www.canadiangeographic.ca/article/animal-facts-snowy-owl

National Geographic Kids, Snowy Owls Profile
https://kids.nationalgeographic.com/animals/snowy-owl/

CRITICAL THINKING QUESTIONS

1. What makes snowy owls different from other owls?

2. What do snowy owls eat?

3. What kinds of threats do snowy owls face?

INDEX